Seeing and praying
The meaning and motivation of Christian discipleship

Steve Bradbury with Allan Harkness

The Changemakers! series is published by Scripture Union and TEAR Australia

Seeing and praying: the meaning and motivation of christian discipleship.
© Scripture Union Australia, 2000

Scripture Union books are published in Australia by
Scripture Union Australia
Resources for Ministry Unit
PO Box 77
Lidcombe
NSW 1825, Australia

Unless otherwise stated, Scriptures quoted are from the *New Revised Standard Version* Bible, © 1989, Division of Christian Education of the National Council of the Churches of Christ in the United States of America. Used by permission.

National Library of Australia Cataloguing-in-Publication Data

Bradbury, Steve.
Seeing and praying: the meaning and motivation of christian discipleship.

ISBN 0 949720 87 9

1. Discipling (Christianity). 2. Poverty - Religious aspects I. Harkness, Allan. II. Scripture Union Australia. III. TEAR Australia. IV. Title. V. Title: Meaning and motivation of christian discipleship. (Series: Changemakers!)

261.832

All rights reserved. No portion of this publication may be reproduced by any means without the written permission of the publisher.

Cover Design and typesetting by
Openbook Publishers, Adelaide, SA.
Cover photo © Tearfund (UK)

CONTENTS

	Page
Introduction	4
Study One: 'If you love me...'	5
Study Two: Worship	10
Study Three: Seek justice	15
Study Four: Praying against injustice	20
Study Five: 'We'll pray – but who for?'	24
Further reading	31

INTRODUCTION

It was at the turbulent age of 14 going on 15 when I made the radical decision to follow Christ, much to the surprise and occasional consternation of my parents.

With this about-turn it was not surprising that I decided to join the large and energetic Scripture Union that made waves in my high school.

Important friendships developed with Christian teachers and peers, and I discovered the richness that ought to characterise Christian fellowship.

It was in this context that I learned of the immense importance of the Bible.

No sooner had I come to faith than I was taught, and believed, that this special book was a manual from God – given to show us how we must live.

That conviction remains with me today, and it explains why I have sweated over this small series of studies.

There are times when it seems to me that nearly every page of the Scriptures contains evidence of God's abiding love for the poor, his deep mercy, and his passion for justice.

My great hope is that this series will encourage many Christians to examine this evidence, and in so doing allow the Holy Spirit to dig deeply into their hearts and minds.

If this were to happen, I couldn't even begin to predict the consequences.

Steve Bradbury
National Director, TEAR Australia

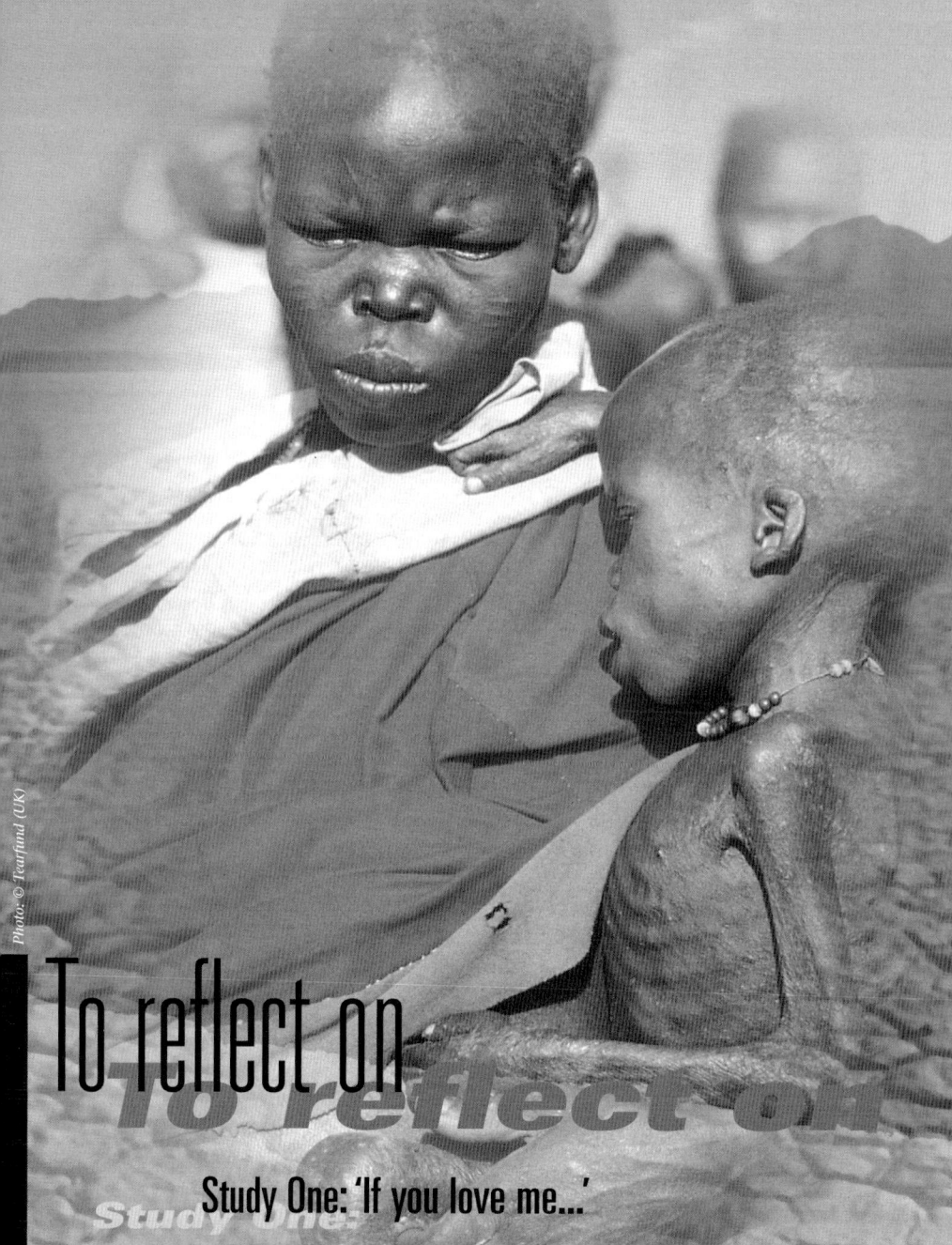

To reflect on

Study One: 'If you love me...'

"When you give a banquet, invite the poor, the crippled, the lame, and the blind. And you will be blessed because they cannot repay you, for you will be repaid at the resurrection of the righteous."
(Luke 14:14)

Study One: IF YOU LOVE ME...

minutes 10-15

Introduction

1. 'Love' is often considered a 'weasel-word', a word that has lost its impact because it is used in so many different ways.
- **Using a large sheet of paper and felt-tip pens, brainstorm with your group on the wide range of different meanings of 'love'.**
- **Allow members to recount humorous or serious situations where they experienced some of the different meanings of 'love'.**

Which meanings had the most significance and which the least?

2. Pray as you move into this study, asking the Spirit to help you understand what you will learn together and to fill you with a deep desire to love and serve God.

3. Read John 14:15-24 together. To increase its impact, have one person read the passage aloud, with appropriate emphasis.

Ask group members to keep the context of the passage in mind: Jesus is rapidly approaching his crucifixion and knows his remaining time with the disciples is limited.

After nearly three years of tutoring them intensively, he will leave them shortly. Then the awesome responsibility of planting and nurturing the soon-to-be established Christian communities will be theirs.

So there is urgency on Jesus' part, and increasing anxiety on the part of his disciples, as he impresses upon them the crucial 'formula' which is at the heart of this passage.

10 minutes

'If you love me...'

1. What are the key features of this 'formula' in John 14:15-24?

2. Implied in the passage is the fact that God wants our love. What does this tell you about the character of God?

3. What does it mean *to you* to be able to say, 'I love Jesus'? Can you relate an experience or incident which can help others in the group appreciate your ideas?

20-25 minutes

'... you will keep my commandments'

1. Identify the places in John 14:15-24 where Jesus links love and obedience. What dynamic did Jesus want his disciples to experience through 'keeping his commandments'?

2. What is God's purpose behind this? (A comparison with the principles of loving parenting may help you find an answer to this question.)

3. Jesus gave numerous commands to his disciples, some clearly of broader significance than others. In your group,

decide on the three to five commands you find most significant. (Matthew 5:14-16; 28:18-20; Luke 14:12-14; John 13:12-17 are possibilities.)

- Divide your group into sub-groups or pairs, with each sub-group taking one of the commands chosen.
- Spend some time considering the implications of the particular command for you as an individual and for your church or small group as a faith community.
- Allow a short time for each sub-group to report their findings. What insights do the different groups have in common?

"When you give a banquet, invite the poor, the crippled, the lame, and the blind. And you will be blessed because they cannot repay you, for you will be repaid at the resurrection of the righteous." (Luke 14:14)

Photo: © Matt Wade TEAR Australia

minutes **20**

The gift of God's Spirit

Assess your ability to fulfil the wonderful vision spelt out in the command you investigated on page 6.

- **How easy or difficult is it to fulfil the requirements of the command?**

Photo: © Matt Wade TEAR Australia

Jesus was fully aware that obedience is not easy so did not leave his disciples then or today, without resources.

1. What such resources are mentioned in John 14:15-24?

2. Look especially at verses 16 and 26. In the original Greek language of the gospels, the word translated 'advocate' (NRSV) or 'counsellor' (NIV) meant someone who takes our side in difficult situations.

This could be a witness who gives evidence on our behalf in a court of law; a person who provides wise advice when it is needed; someone who comforts us when we are distressed.

- **Knowing these meanings, what is the relevance to the disciples of Jesus' promise that God will give them the Holy Spirit, and his call for them to obey his commands?**

3. At the time Jesus made his promise, the disciples did not fully understand its significance.

- **Look up another promise Jesus made then that was to have a more immediate impact (verses 18-19).**

Imagine you were one of Jesus' disciples. Knowing this promise, describe how it might have affected you in the following 2-3 months (from the time of the arrest and death of Jesus through to his ascension and the Pentecost events).

4. As individuals, think quietly about the importance of the Holy Spirit in your life.

- **Have you had any experience of the Holy Spirit's role in enabling you to fulfil the commands of Jesus?**

- **Are you able to identify times when the Holy Spirit has come to you in any of the three ways outlined above?**

- **Encourage members to share their insights. (Note: this is a time for careful and loving listening, rather than for theological debate!)**

minutes **10**

Notes:

Conclusion

Reflect on the importance of the passage you have explored in this study.
- **Is there a particular encouragement or challenge you can share with the group?**

As a group, turn the thoughts of the study into prayer.
- **Ask Jesus to deepen each member's relationship with him.**
- **Ask for it to be expressed in their greater love and obedience to him.**
- **Invite the Holy Spirit to work in the lives of both individuals, the group and their church(es) that they will be open to his initiatives and presence.**
- **If it is appropriate, sing prayerfully songs the group knows that address the Holy Spirit.**

Until your next meeting

- **Each day, set aside some time to recollect Jesus' promise to his disciples – that they will receive the help of the Advocate in their efforts to obey his commands.**

Review your attitudes and behaviour and how they are changing.

Keep a journal or diary to help this process. (See appendix for journal writing references.)

Preparation for the next study

A poster size sheet of paper will be needed for the next study, and some felt-tip pens.

Photo: © Tearfund (UK) and Matt Wade TEAR Australia

To reflect on

Study Two: Worship

'Each Sunday millions of Christians worldwide gather together in a multitude of congregations to worship the one true God.'
Steve Bradbury

WORSHIP

Introduction

1. Spend the first few minutes talking together about perspectives on discipleship.
- **What are the results of any efforts to apply the insights of the first study?**
- **Have any of your previous views changed?**

Rejoice with those who have been encouraged, empathise with those who have struggles or feel they have failed in some way.

Use these shared experiences as a basis for prayer for each other.
- **Ask the Holy Spirit to teach you in this study – and for your lives to be open to shaping by the Spirit.**

2. Each Sunday millions of Christians worldwide gather together in a multitude of congregations to worship the one true God.
- **What do you think would happen if this practice suddenly stopped?**
- **Would anyone outside these gatherings notice the difference?**

This study is an opportunity to expose your understanding and practice of worship to the scrutiny of Bible teaching.

It will help you think about how your worship activities relate to the society around you, both local and global, and encourage you to ask about the purpose of these weekly events.

'Lovely service, vicar'

Read the following comments.

'That was a great time of worship, I could really sense God's presence.'

'Why do we have to sing so many choruses and songs in our worship? They just goes on and on.'

'If only our worship services could always be as good as today's. The sermon and the music were fantastic.'

'I can't help but feel that everything we did and said in our worship today was basically irrelevant.'

(add similar comments that group members have heard recently)

- **Think about your most meaningful experience of worship in the past few months.**
Why was it so special to you?
- **Share your thoughts with the rest of the group. Identify any common features that members of your group value or appreciate about worshipping with others.**

Seeing and Praying 11

- From the group's experience, how would most Christians in your community sum up the value of a particular worship service?
- List the ideas, and then determine which would be the leading 3-4 standards used.

Silently read these two comments:

'It is far too easy, within the current upsurge of creative input in the realm of worship, to find ourselves chasing spiritual or aesthetic experiences, as if the highest achievement of our whole pilgrimage on earth was to enter some kind of praise-induced ecstasy.'

Graham Kendrick

'I wonder sometimes whether it is worship we worship, whether what we experience in music and song is actually our primary motivation, rather than honour of God.'

Barry Chant

1. What fundamental issue is raised by these quotations?

2. To what extent do these comments reflect your experience of congregational worship?
- **Is self-absorption a problem?**
- **If you have been able to view different worship traditions (for example, 'charismatic', Pentecostal, meditative or liturgical worship forms), have you ever observed any examples of 'self-absorption' problems in them?**
- **Is self-absorption a danger whatever the tradition of worship?**

'Thus says the Lord' ... back then

Read Isaiah 1:10-17; Amos 5:21-24; and Micah 6:1-8. (These passages could be read aloud in the group. Alternatively, divide into three smaller groups, each taking one passage.)

How do each of these passages answer the following questions:

1. What worship was being offered to God?

2. What sort of language does God use to criticise them?

3. Why was God so dissatisfied with their worship? What was lacking?

Pool the answers from all three passages. What common threads do you discover?

See Matthew 15:3-9, where Jesus cites similar passages.

'Thus says the Lord' ... to us, today?

Do the words spoken by prophets such as Isaiah, Amos and Micah so many years ago have any relevance to your church situation today?

1. Imagine yourself as Isaiah, Amos or Micah. You are coming into a worship service of your church. What message would you want to bring from God?

- **Take a few minutes to jot down ideas for what you would say.**

- Update this message for today and re-write one of the passages above.

(Some of the language will remain much the same, but other aspects will require significant change, unless animal sacrifices are part of your worship!)

Try to retain a similar tone and urgency to what is in the original text.

- Take turns to 'proclaim' your message to the rest of the group. (Do not allow discussion until after all members have had their turn.)

2. Discuss together how much you believe these 'contemporary messages' are on target for your specific church situation.

How well would messages of this kind go down in your church? For the message to get across, what changes would need to be made to the form and content of your worship services?

3. Suggest some practical steps which you, either individually and/or as a group, could take to more effectively reflect God's concerns as expressed through the prophetic words studied in this session.

Write these in the space below.

 *10 minutes*

Conclusion

1. Have each person make up a newspaper headline summarising the message of this study. Write out each headline on an A3 size sheet or strip of paper using felt-tip pens. Display the contributions.

2. Use these headlines as a focus for quiet reflection on the study and its impact for you and your church.

3. Set aside a time for group prayer and/or worship. Pray specifically for your church and its leaders that your congregational worship will reflect God's perspectives.

If you like, read together the hymn from Sri Lanka found on next page.

Conclude by saying the Lord's Prayer together.

Until your next meeting

'Involvement in God's mission of justice in the world provides the necessary context for the true worship of God.'

Athol Gill

Use this quotation as a basis for reflection and for assessing the worship events you attend between your meeting times.

Be prepared to comment on your insights at the next meeting.

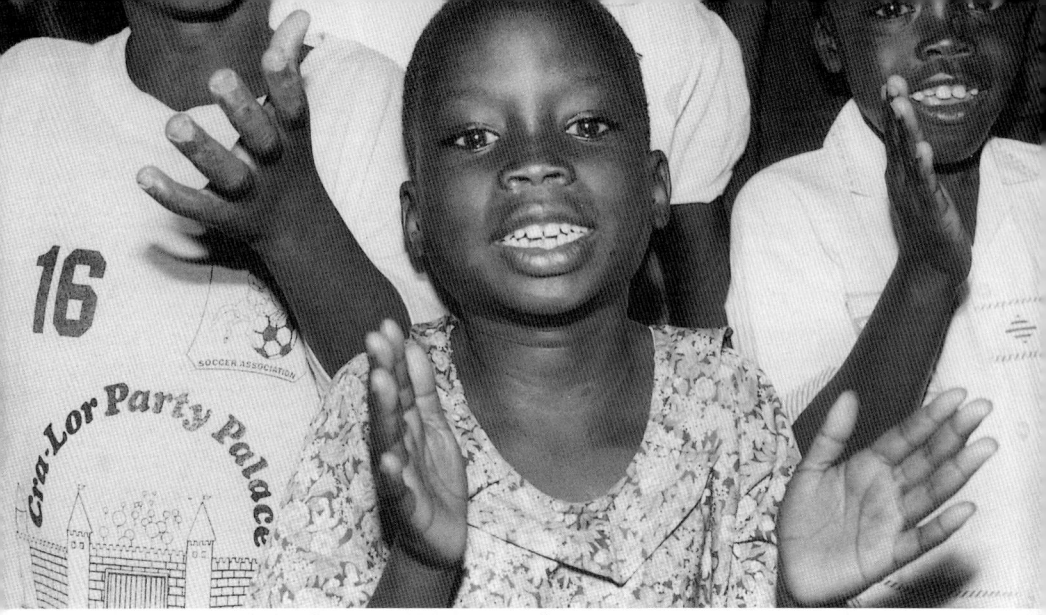

Raising our hands as a sign of rejoicing. Photo: © Matt Wade TEAR Australia

Refrain:

Worship the Lord, worship the Father, the Spirit, the Son,
raising our hands in devotion to him who is one.

Raising our hands as a sign of rejoicing
and with our lips our togetherness voicing,
giving ourselves to a life of creativeness.
Worship and work must be one!

Praying and training that we be a blessing
and by our workmanship daily expressing
we are committed to serving humanity.
Worship and work must be one!

Called to be partners with God in creation,
honouring Christ as the Lord of the nation,
we must be ready for risk and for sacrifice.
Worship and work must be one!

Now, in response to the life you are giving,
help us, O Father, to offer our living,
seeking a just and a healing society.
Worship and work must be one!

Fred Kaan, words © 1990 Stainer & Bell Ltd, London, UK, permission sought.

Preparation for the next session

• For one exercise you will need enough felt-tip pens for members to have one each, and three large sheets of paper.

• Small pieces of light card suitable for bookmarks.

• Resources on different courses of action that people can take to seek justice. See the areas suggested in the section, 'Seeking justice in a world of injustice' (Study Three, p. 18).

To reflect on

Study Three: Seek justice

"The field of the poor may yield much food,
but it is swept away by injustice."
Proverbs 13:23

Study Three: SEEK JUSTICE

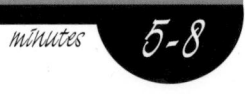
minutes 5-8

Introduction

Review the last study. Listen carefully as each of you recounts some of your thinking and experiences since you last met.

Take time to pray for what has been shared together – both the positive and more challenging concerns.

minutes 15

Justice? – 'It's not fair!'

You hear these words spoken as an assertive shout, a defeated mumble or to register disapproval of a wrong suffered. When did you last hear someone voice them?

Children seem to develop at least a very basic concept of justice at an early age; and adults become adept at recognising when justice is absent – at least where an injustice affects them directly.

The previous study showed the relationship between worship and justice.

If our worship is to be acceptable to God, obeying the command to 'seek justice' must be a basic part of our lives. But what does this mean in practice.

This study gives us opportunity to examine what the Bible tells us about justice, and to consider what it means to actively seek it.

1. Describe to one another your worst, or most recent experience of injustice – something you yourself experienced or witnessed.

2. On three large sheets of paper, write the following questions on the paper using felt-tip pens:
• Sheet One:
   What does the word 'justice' mean?
• Sheet Two:
   Why is justice important to any society?
• Sheet Three:
   What are the obstacles to justice?

Then *either*, brainstorm together on these questions, recording all the group's ideas without discussion,

Or, give members felt-tip pens, allowing them to write on the sheets as ideas come to mind.

(NB: it is not necessary to use Bible references in this exercise.)

3. Let the whole group look at the completed sheets, then circle ideas and concepts the group considers most important.

20-25 minutes

Developing a biblical definition

1. Allocate the following Bible passages to group members:
Deuteronomy 16:18-20; Deuteronomy 24:10-15,17-22; Isaiah 10:1-2; Isaiah 58:1-9; Jeremiah 22:13-17;

Micah 2:1-2 (plus Proverbs 13:23); Amos 5:10-12; James 5:1-4.

2. For each passage

- **On a sheet of paper, write a short definition (no more than 15 words) of the concept of justice.**
- **Make a list of the people identified as being in need of justice.**

3. Report the various discoveries to the whole group.

4. Evaluate these findings against the life and teaching of Jesus.

- **Discuss whether these discoveries 'ring true' in terms of the Good News he proclaimed and demonstrated. In what ways?**

It is not always easy to understand how we should apply Old Testament teaching in today's world but we need to remember that Jesus had enormous respect for the Old Testament scriptures (Matthew 5:17-20).

Also, as Christopher Wright points out in the preface of his excellent book, *Living as the People of God*, 'It was the Old Testament that the Apostle Paul had in mind when he spoke of the double purpose of the Scriptures.

Not only are they able to bring people to saving faith…but they have a continuing ethical validity.' (2 Tim. 3:15-17)

Read these two quotations:

'The tears of God are the soil in which his love of justice is rooted.'

Nicholas Wolterstorff

'The provisions of justice for the needy are the expressions of God's compassion for the weak and God's hostility to oppression.'

Stephen Mott

In the Bible passages you have been examining, what evidence can you find to support the claims of Wolterstorff and Mott?

Photo: © Tearfund (UK)

10 minutes

Apply your discoveries

Read this case study:

In the eastern Ugandan district of Kumi, a local community drew on help from TEAR to develop a special nursery for a virus-resistant cassava*.

Previous crops of cassava, the staple food in the region, had been wiped out by disease, causing considerable hardship throughout the region.

Once the nursery cassava reached maturity it was to be harvested, and the roots divided and distributed for planting throughout the community.

However, in the months before harvest many people in the community were severely affected by drought.

Some began to steal from the nursery in order to feed their families.

When he was asked what he was doing to prevent further stealing, the man responsible for the nursery answered, 'It would be wrong for us to try and stop them.

It is better to steal than to starve.'

*cassava, a root crop, is the staple food in Kumi.

Imagine you are a group of Christian leaders in the church in Kumi.

In the light of your discoveries about biblical justice so far in this study, how would you respond to this comment?

10 minutes

Seeking justice in a world of injustice

It is one thing to know the biblical perspective on justice – but quite another to decide what it means in practice to seek justice for the poor and oppressed in our world.

Think about the following possible courses of action:

1. *Participation in national and international advocacy programs that promote justice for the poor.*

(e.g. campaigns which address issues like baby food, Third World debt, child labour and human rights). What programs of this kind are you aware of? Talk about the involvement of group members in such actions? How meaningful and effective are they?

2. *Re-allocation of resources over which we personally exercise some control.*

What range of resources comes into this category? Talk about the variety of processes or channels of re-allocation that can be used. What difference can this make to poor and oppressed communities?

3. *'Immersion in the problems of this world leads us to seek new depths in prayer and a more concrete and robust spirituality' (Roy McCloughry).*

Talk together about how easy or how difficult you find it to pray on behalf of those who are oppressed by injustice? What resources or methods have you found helpful in praying this type of prayer? (NB: the next study explores this subject in more detail.)

4. What other courses of action can group members suggest?

- Select one course of action to experiment with either individually or with others in the coming weeks. Pool suggestions with one or two other group members about practical steps you could take to assist you to do something in your chosen area.
- Encourage members to complete this sentence, 'By our next meeting I/we hope to have … … …'.

Get them to write it out on the card supplied to make a small bookmark. Invite them to share their response with the group.

[It may be more informative for the group if each of the general areas of action mentioned above is selected by one person or more. However, don't force any option onto members.]

Resources

Information that can help you engage in actions and prayer for justice can be obtained from TEAR Australia, Tearfund and Amnesty International. You could also contact denominational and inter-denominational domestic welfare agencies.

minutes 8-10

Conclusion

Conclude this study with specific prayer. You may wish to follow this order:

1. Start by praying this prayer from Iona:

*Lead me O God
on the journey of justice
Guide me O God
on the pathways of peace
Renew me O God
by the wellspring of grace*
Today, tonight and forever.
Celtic Prayers from Iona, reproduced by permission. © J. Philip Newell, Paulist Press, 1997, USA

2. Have a time of free prayer, praying specifically for:

- situations of injustice known to members (both nearby and distant),
- each member to be increasingly sensitised to God's concerns for justice,
- the resources and guidance of the Holy Spirit for the commitments to action which members wrote out on their bookmarks.

3. Conclude by repeating the Iona prayer, changing 'me' to 'us' if appropriate.

Until your next meeting:

Keep your bookmark where you will see it often (e.g. in your Bible or wallet; on the bathroom mirror, etc). Use it to remind you to work on your area of action.

At the start of each day, pray the Iona prayer. At each day's end, review where you have seen God 'leading… guiding… and renewing' you.

Preparation for the next study:

During the study (see p. 22) you will require information and photographs of one or more current oppressive situations in your country and elsewhere in the world. Possible sources are aid and development organisations, newspapers and current affairs magazines.

Decide whether all the group members will focus on the same situation or several situations. This will determine the number of multiple copies of the photograph(s) required.

To reflect on

Study Four: Pray for the weak and oppressed

"God presides in the great assembly; he gives judgement among the 'gods': 'How long will you defend the unjust and show partiality to the wicked? Defend the cause of the weak and fatherless; maintain the rights of the poor and oppressed. Rescue the weak and needy; deliver them from the hand of the wicked.'" **Psalm 82:1-4 (NIV)**

Study Four: PRAYING AGAINST INJUSTICE

minutes 10

Introduction

Encourage members to take time to catch up on what has happened in their lives since the last study.

- **Since praying the Iona prayer regularly, have members become more aware that God has been 'leading ... guiding ... renewing' them? In which specific areas?**
- **What challenges have members faced in the different areas of action written on the bookmarks last study? Review progress and/or failures.**

Allow your discussion to lead into prayer together.

minutes 10

Praying for others – a challenge!

In his great classic, *Prayer*, Ole Hallesby wrote: 'I think we all admit, both to ourselves and to others, without any question, that to pray is difficult.'

Is this your experience? If many Christians find *most* prayer difficult, then you probably find praying with – and on behalf of – the victims of injustice, even more so.

Take a few minutes to check this out in your group:

1. How regularly do members pray about the suffering of the weak and oppressed?

2. How often are such prayers said in your church?

3. Why do you think most of us find prayer of this kind difficult?

20-25 minutes

Smash their teeth!

Ask one person to read Psalm 58 aloud, then have 2-3 minutes of silence to individually reflect on what has just been heard.

This prayer is not easy reading for the sensitive or squeamish because it is full of anger – anger directed at those who use their power and authority to maliciously exploit the weak. The conditions described by the psalmist have been common throughout human history.

Today millions of people are still on the receiving end of the oppression described in verse 2, making this prayer as relevant today as when it was first written.

Discuss the following questions:

1. What do verses 1-5 tell about the nature of oppression?
- **Describe the oppressors.**
- **How does oppression come about?**

(See Job 24:1-12 for a more detailed description of oppression.)

2. Read aloud again verses 6-9, letting the ideas determine the tone and emphasis used. What impact do these words have on you? Why are you affected in this way?

Seeing and Praying 21

3. Try and place yourself in the position of a downtrodden person, such as a poor labourer (James 5:4) or a victim of oppression (Job 24:1-12). As the oppressed person, how might you feel about the psalmist's request to God?

4. In what areas does the teaching of Jesus reinforce the thrust of the psalmist's prayer? (If the group cannot come up with suggestions, use the time between now and your next study to do some research, then report back at the beginning of the next study.)

5. Coming back to your own situation, what significance do your insights have on these questions about how to pray against injustice? Relate your thoughts back to the answers given to the questions in the section above, 'Praying for others – a challenge!'. What strategies could you adopt to help overcome the difficulties expressed?

6. Suggest specific ideas for inclusion in prayer for people and communities that are victims of injustice. Choose ones that would be meaningful for group members.

Prayer and reflection

'The best way to learn about praying is to pray.'

[Note: Have on hand some relevant data you have gathered, including photographs of current situations where oppression exists.

Sources of useful information are literature supplied by aid and development organisations, newspapers and current affairs magazines.

Make sure the photographs show poverty and struggle, but remember they don't have to be too harrowing to make the point.]

Use the full time you have available to pray for those experiencing harsh oppression and injustice. As you do pray, remember God's deep concern for the poor and oppressed. So long as you do not turn a blind eye and a deaf ear to their suffering, the Holy Spirit will enable you to pray for them.

To assist the prayer process,

Either make sure each person in the group has information on the same situation and a copy of the same photograph,

Or, divide into smaller groups of two or three people, with each sub-group praying for a different situation.

- **Step One: Study the data and photo carefully. Keep any discussion brief – use it for clarification, not debate.**

- **Step Two: Sit or kneel with the photo in front of you. Ask the Holy Spirit to help you identify with these nameless, suffering people.**

If you were them, what would you feel? How would you cope? What would you do? Who would you turn to for help? What would you say to God?

- **Step Three: Pray** *for* **these people and** *with* **them. Don't worry if your prayer isn't polished and articulate.**

Recognise that through prayer it is possible for a little of their pain to seep into you, thus allowing our voices, our groans and our tears to be joined to theirs.

Don't worry if you are not sure how to pray, or if you need to remain silent. Remember that there are always times when *'we do not know how to pray as we ought, but that very Spirit intercedes with sighs too deep for words. And God, who searches the heart, knows what is the mind of the Spirit, because the Spirit intercedes for the saints according to the will of God.'* (Romans 8:26b-27)

Photo: © Darryl & Lyn Jackson TEAR Australia

'He prayed as he breathed, forming no words and making no specific requests, only holding in his heart, like broken birds in cupped hands, all those people who were in stress or grief.'

Ellis Peters

Conclude your time of prayer by saying the Lord's Prayer together, or quietly singing an appropriate song/songs.

Until your next meeting:

• **Take time to think about what you prayed for in the study.**

How might God want you to express your active partnership with him in answer to your prayer?

How might you continue to pray for injustice?

Note ideas, and explore avenues for action.

• **An exercise to consider: As you read the newspaper or watch TV news broadcasts, ask for help to see what is happening from God's perspective.**

Consciously pray about the situations you see reported. Be ready to share your discoveries when you meet next with your group.

'To pray is to change. Prayer is the central avenue God uses to transform us. If we are unwilling to change, we will abandon prayer as a noticeable characteristic of our lives....

In prayer, real prayer, we begin to think God's thoughts after Him: to desire the things He desires, to love the things He loves. Progressively we are taught to see things from His point of view.'

Richard Foster

Preparation for the next study:

You will need a large sheet of paper and felt-tip pens for one component of the study (page 28). Write out the text required before your meeting.

For the suggested song on page 30, if you think the group or an individual will want to sing it, locate the music for it.

Notes:

Photo: © Darryl & Lyn Jackson TEAR Australia

To reflect on

Study Five: 'We'll pray, but who for?'

'Show us how to serve the neighbours we have from you.'
From a folk song from Ghana – Chereponi

Study Five: 'WE'LL PRAY, BUT WHO FOR?'

minutes 8-10

Introduction

Allow time for members to report on their activities and discoveries since the last meeting. Talk about any concerns that have arisen for members as they have tried to pray more effectively for those affected by injustice or through seeing the world more and more from God's perspective. Take time to pray for these matters then commit this study to God, asking especially that you may be open to God's surprises!

Accept surprises
That upset your plans,
Shatter your dreams,
Give a completely
Different turn
to your day
and – who knows? –
to your life.
It is not chance.
Leave the Father free
Himself to weave
the pattern of your days.

Dom Helder Camara, *A Thousand Reasons for Living,* Darton, Longman and Todd, 1981, p. 92 (Permission sought).

minutes 5

Neighbours?
Who are my neighbours?

It's one thing to get fired up to pray for those who are oppressed but how do you overcome the sense of distance between you and those for whom you are praying when you are unlikely to ever meet them.

How do you move forward?

Everyone has neighbours and is a neighbour.

Whether you live in a high-rise building with many apartments, in a street of several households within shouting distance, or in the bush or countryside with the nearest household kilometres away, you still live with neighbours.

What people mean by being 'good' neighbours or having 'good' neighbours varies.

For some, being a 'good' neighbour means being isolationist – keeping to yourself, causing no bother, never making demands.

For others, 'good' means having some acceptable level of involvement.

• **Quickly go around the members of the group. Allow each person to say whether they have 'good', 'bad' or 'indifferent' neighbours. On what basis they have made this judgement?**

10-15 minutes

The greatest command

This story of the compassionate Samaritan, a parable of Jesus, provides some surprising clues about what it means to be a good neighbour.

Jesus spells out clearly for us that our relationship with our neighbours is

Seeing and Praying 25

inextricably intertwined with our relationship with God.

Read Luke 10:25-37.

1. Note the first question the lawyer asked Jesus (v.25). Suggest why this might have been an issue for the lawyer.

- **In today's world, when are people most likely to show interest in 'eternal life'?**
- **How might they ask questions that show they are interested in this?**

2. Jesus is a superb teacher. See how he gets the lawyer to answer his own question (vv.26-28).

- **Spend some time 'unpacking' the meaning of what is often called the 'greatest commandment' (Deuteronomy 10:12-22; John 14:15-24; and 1 John 4:19-21 provide additional insights).**

3. Think of the range of ways you have demonstrated your love for God in the last few weeks?

- **What similarities and differences are there between how we express our love for God and for those around us (e.g. parent, child, sibling, partner, friend, etc.)?**

4. What possible reasons might Luke have had for suggesting that the lawyer 'wanted to justify himself' (v.29)?

'Jesus' teaching is that eternal life begins here and now and is a present reality as well as a future hope.

'There is thus a continuity between life now and life to come.

'This life begins when a believer accepts Jesus' offer of salvation and is given the Holy Spirit, and it is deepened as the Christian encounters the risen power of the Lord.'

George Carey, 'Finding Faith', in *An Introduction to the Christian Faith*, Lynx, 1992, p. 232

15-20 minutes

Loving our neighbour

1. Focus for a few minutes on the Samaritan. List the things he did and the likely significance of each.

- **What did it cost the Samaritan? (Hint: don't think only in terms of money.)**

2. Both the priest and Levite in the story failed to respond to the needs of the robbed and beaten stranger.

- **They probably had good reasons for not responding – suggest what these reasons were most likely to be.**

3. In this story, Jesus deliberately chose an unlikely hero.

- **From your understanding of historic relationships between Jew and Samaritan, what do you think the lawyer would have felt when he heard the story?**
- **Is there a principle you can transfer from this to your own 'neighbour' responsibilities?**

(NB. Poor relations between Samaritans and Jews are rooted in the mass deportations of Northern Kingdom Jews to Assyria after the fall of Samaria in 720 BC and the reverse deportations of people from Babylonia, Hamath and other places, who were forced to settle in Samaria.

Naturally they brought their customs and religions with them. With time they mingled with those Israelites not taken into exile.

Their descendants came to be known as 'Samaritans'. Jews returning after the exile followed the teaching laid down by Ezra.

They viewed the religious practices of the Samaritans as tainted and thus despised them and refrained from any contact with them.)

4. Imagine the lawyer asked you to help him understand Jesus' story.

'I asked Jesus, "And who is my neighbour?" but I couldn't understand what he meant.' Can you give him a brief answer?

5. William Barclay, a noted Christian writer has stressed that any person anywhere in the world who is in need is our neighbour, and that 'our help must be as wide as the love of God'.

Photo: © TEAR Australia

- **How realistic and how important is this claim for Christians today?**

6. Think of your immediate neighbours and share what you think their needs are.

- **Do you sometimes find this a difficult question to answer?**
- **Why?**
- **What could be done to change this?**

7. All of us are often unresponsive to the needs of others, whether they are near and distant?

- **Why do you think this is?**

8. A committed response to the needs of our neighbours will probably lead to questions about what causes those needs.

- **Why do questions of this kind often disturb us?**

minutes 15-20

How to respond?

1. There is no way we can respond to every need we become aware of, either as individuals or as small groups.

- **How should we determine our priorities?**

(Note: you may want to refer back to insights from the earlier studies in this book as you answer this question)

2. Congregations are better placed to respond more comprehensively to the needs of both local and global neighbours.

- **Draw up a chart similar to this.**

Brainstorm together on some of the practical steps your congregation is taking, or could take, to ensure that the needs of your local and global neighbours are not neglected.

Practical steps being taken in response to the needs of our ***local*** neighbours

_____
_____
_____
_____
_____
_____
_____

Practical steps being taken in response to the needs of our ***global*** neighbours

_____
_____
_____
_____
_____
_____
_____
_____

- **Which box has the most items and which the least?**
- **What might this indicate?**

In your group, highlight one area in the 'practical steps being taken' boxes that could be realistically and actively pursued by your group.

Discuss whether you are willing and able to respond to it, and what course of action needs to be set.

As you discuss, keep these questions in mind:

- **Given your family, church and work commitments, what time and energy is left for a neighbour in need?**

- **Is there a need for some re-ordering of existing priorities so that you can more fully respond to God's command to 'love your neighbour as yourself'?**

Photo: © TEAR Australia

minutes 10

Conclusion

To prepare for prayer to conclude this study, reflect upon your discoveries above, and...

Read the following:

'We dare not forget that the very ones who missed the opportunity of ministry in our Lord's story were two very 'religious' men... So busy were they in the performance of their religious routine that they had no time for even a cursory examination of the stricken man.'

Art Beals

"Jesus asked Peter, 'Do you love me?'"
- **If Jesus asked you this question now, what answer would you give?**

Pray together

- **Use insights from this study to give direction to your prayer, including any local and global needs.**
- **Ask for guidance about how you should respond to those needs.**
- **Conclude your prayer by saying or singing this song:**

Fill us with your love

Kneels at the feet of his friends,
Silently washes their feet;
Master who acts as a slave to them.

Chorus:
Yesu, Yesu, fill us with your love,
Show us how to serve
The neighbours we have from you.

Neighbours are rich men and poor,
Neighbours are black men and white;
Neighbours are nearby and far away.

These are the ones we should serve,
These are the ones we should love;
all men are neighbours to us and you.

Loving puts us on our knees,
Serving as though we are slaves;
This is the way we should live with you.

Chereponi – Ghana folk song adapted by Tom Colvin – words © 1969 Agape/Hope Publishing Company. Administered in Australasia by The Nightlight Music Group. Reproduced by permission.

If this is the last planned meeting of your group:
- **Take time to review the studies in this book.**
- **What has been most significant for you? Most encouraging? Most disturbing? Most challenging?**
- **Encourage each other to make a covenant with God and/or with each other to apply the discoveries you have made.**
- **Choose something that will be relevant to your situation.**
- **The appendix gives suggestions about possible avenues to explore for action.**

Until your next meeting

Consider making a commitment to pray this prayer each day until your next group meeting: 'Lord Jesus, show me today someone I can call "neighbour" and some way of serving that person'.

- **Note what you discover.**
- **If you have identified an area of action for your congregation or your small group, make informal contact with others who are also involved so you can encourage and support each other.**

This will help you to keep your resolve alive.

FURTHER READING

Introductory

Andrews, Dave
  Can You Hear the Heartbeat (Hodder and Stoughton, 1989)
Rand, Stephen
  Guinea Pig For Lunch (Hodder and Stoughton, 1998)
Sider, R.
  Rich Christians in an Age of Hunger (Hodder and Stoughton, 1997)
Stott, J.
  Issues Facing Christians Today, 2nd Edition (HarperCollins, 1990)

More Advanced

Grigg, V.
  Companion to the Poor (Albatross, 1984)
Haugen, Gary A.
  Good News About Injustice (IVP, 1999)
Hughes, Dewi
  God of the Poor (OM, 1998)
Wallis, Jim
  The Soul of Politics (Harper Collins, 1995)
Wright, C.J.H.
  Living As The People Of God (IVP, 1983)

A wide range of relevant educational resources, including videos, magazines, information packs, youth and children's materials are available from **TEAR Australia and Tearfund.**

Contact Details

TEAR Australia
P.O. Box 289
Hawthorn 3122
Australia
Phone: (03) 9819 1900 or Toll Free 1800 244 986 Fax: (03) 9818 3586
E-mail: tearaust@tear.org.au   Web site: www.tear.org.au

Tearfund
100 Church Road
Teddington, Middlesex TW11 8QE
United Kingdom
Phone: 0845 355 8355 Fax: (0)181 943 3594
E-mail: enquiry@tearfund.dircon.co.uk   Web site: www.tearfund.org